Come to the Fair
by Audree Distad

"Have you ever visited a state fair? Been dazzled by the rides and the noise, the color and motion? Come along now... come to the fair!"

Each year all around the country, young people wait impatiently for the state fair. Wait for the chance to show the pigs or sheep they have raised themselves; to watch the rodeo and ride the Ferris wheel; to cook a prizewinning dish.

There's Marty—who scrubs and combs his sheep until they are fluffy enough to catch the judge's eye and win a purple ribbon. There's LaMona who, after hours and hours of practice, puts on her white chaps and blue-checkered shirt and proudly rides her horse Dolly into the show ring.

Come meet Marty and LaMona and the other boys and girls who invite everyone to "Come to the Fair!"

COME
TO THE
FAIR

COME
TO THE
FAIR

by AUDREE DISTAD

Harper & Row, Publishers
New York, Hagerstown, San Francisco, London

COME TO THE FAIR
Copyright © 1977 by Audree Distad

FIRST EDITION

Library of Congress Cataloging in Publication Data
Distad, Audree.
    Come to the fair.

    SUMMARY: Follows several youngsters as they participate in the contests and exhibi-tions of a state fair.
        1. South Dakota State Fair, Huron, S.D.—Juvenile literature.   2. 4-H clubs—
South Dakota—Juvenile literature.   [1. 4-H clubs.   2. Agricultural exhibitions.
3. Fairs]   I. Title.
S555.S82H83 1977   630′.74′083274   77-3812
ISBN 0-06-021686-7
ISBN 0-06-021687-5 lib. bdg.

For Craig, who loves a fair

CONTENTS

COME
TO THE
FAIR

1

"To the fair in the heart of the country . . ."

Late summer and hot days on the high northern plains. Oats and barley and flax and wheat are cut and combined and trucked to grain elevators and bins. The air shimmers with dust and chaff that stings the throat. Sunflowers and goldenrod line the ditches.

A prairie falcon waits on a haystack for a field mouse to scurry past and become supper. A pheasant strides across the road, russet tail bobbing, hunting the stubble for scattered grain. Harvest month, and time for the State Fair. Time to celebrate.

On farms and ranches all across the country, boys and girls clean and curry livestock, pick and can garden crops, sew clothes and sand furniture, gather rocks and insects, practice speeches and make plans. The wind along the fence rows seems to hum with excitement. It's too long to wait. State Fair . . . coming soon.

Have you ever visited a state fair? Been dazzled by the rides and the noise, the color and motion? Come along now. Let's go to the fair.

Let's go to a state fair in one of our large heartland states—South Dakota. It's not the oldest—the New York State Fair began in 1841; it's not the biggest—the Texas State Fair draws over three million visitors; but it's folksy and fun, and during its six-day run the crowds equal about half the state's population. It is a traditional country fair, with the emphasis on agriculture and livestock—which is natural in a state where the cattle outnumber the people seven to one.

As a fair it began over ninety years ago, when the area was still Dakota Territory, not many years after the Sioux held their last fall powwow at Bear Butte near the Black Hills. A powwow, like a fair, brought everyone together to exchange news, to compete with each other, and to enjoy themselves. Today there are thirty-two hundred state and county fairs in the United States and eight hundred in Canada. Close to 150 million Americans attend fairs each year.

Visiting a fair is fun, but taking part is even better. Marty chooses the sheep and pigs he will show. Shelly hopes to earn a purple ribbon for her cooking. LaMona puts her horse Dolly through practice sessions to prepare her for the ring. John swings his lariat to sharpen his arm. These fairgoers, who live in South Dakota, will share a bit of their world with you.

Most live on working farms (of about 300 to 1,500 acres), others in country homes on a few acres, and some in small

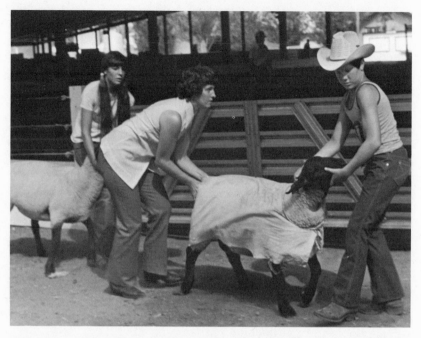

Unloading some projects at the fair takes a full day of pulling and pushing at the 4-H livestock pens. The stylish "jacket" keeps the sheep clean for competition.

towns. Many are members of local 4-H clubs, which take part in the fair. No longer strictly a rural organization, 4-H has about three million members in the United States, all between nine and nineteen years old. Their motto is "Learn by doing," and everyone has at least one project during the year. A member may choose to raise a pig, or make a dress, or cook a casserole, or train a dog—or there are dozens of other choices.

Besides projects, the clubs stress leadership and citizenship. Their symbol is a four-leaf clover with an *H* on every petal. Each *H* is found in the club pledge: "I pledge my *head* to clearer thinking, my *heart* to greater loyalty, my *hands* to larger service, and my *health* to better living for my club, my community and my country." Local clubs meet each month with adult leaders, and often junior leaders, some as young as fourteen. Meetings are not all work—there are picnics and Christmas caroling and a club tour to view members' projects, perhaps a garden or a dairy cow.

Most club members (nicknamed 4-H'ers) enter several projects for the county fair, or a county "achievement day" judging. Everyone hopes for a purple ribbon, the top prize, which will qualify them for the state fair. There will be nearly five thousand 4-H'ers at this state fair alone, bringing with them fifteen thousand exhibits.

Long before a state fair opens, the planning begins. Eleven months is not too long to prepare—almost as soon as the livestock are loaded for the trip home from one fair and the merry-go-round is on its way to another town, preparation begins for next year's fair. The South Dakota fair ends on Labor Day. As early as October, a committee books entertainers for the grandstand show the following year. It takes a busy five months more to line up concessionaires and exhibitors. Tickets must be printed, stalls repaired, workers hired.

South Dakota's fairground of 170 acres sprawls along the edge of the town of Huron, which is a shopping center for farms and small towns, home to a college, and host to stockmen's meetings and basketball tournaments. But while committees work, exhibit halls and barns at the fairground are dark and empty. The grandstand waits. Only the wind wanders there.

And then just weeks before the fair, a stir of activity begins. Bales of yellow straw are unloaded at the barns. Each stall receives a fresh rectangular bundle. It will provide clean bedding for the animals, a nibble if they are hungry, even a welcome place for tired visitors to sit. The air is scented with the sweet hay. Swallows move into the high, dark eaves of the barns, hunting flies and spiders.

The grounds are marked for exhibitors. Here will be the corn pickers . . . there the towering tractors with eight massive wheels . . . beyond a new breed of buffalo-beef cattle. And farther on, a giant lift, the Haybuster, will raise fat round bales of hay weighing up to one thousand pounds. All the week of the fair, farmers will stroll here and there, stop, look, study, compare and ask questions.

Farm equipment manufacturers will show their latest models. A farmer may order a new silo, or arrange for a machinery demonstration on his farm, or explore new feeding methods that could mean fatter cattle. Everyone asks and learns and swaps information—it's why fairs came into being.

Crews arrive on the grounds to set up rows of striped canvas tents for the exhibits. To hold the tents, workmen drive thick metal pegs into the ground, and the clank of sledgehammers echoes across the grounds.

In one large building, a staff prepares the 4-H dormitory. Bunk rooms are swept, mattresses unrolled onto double-deck steel cots, fourteen bunks to a room. Windows are washed and polished; kitchen stoves cleaned and refrigerators stocked; rows of tables and chairs set for hungry girls and boys. Just the place to see old friends and meet new ones. There will be between three hundred and four hundred staying in the dorm. Before campers became popular, the dorm housed fifteen hundred during fair week.

Some judging begins even before the crowds arrive. Two days before the fair opens, county agents from every part of the state arrive, bringing the nonlivestock 4-H exhibits from their areas. Each entry has won a purple ribbon at the county level. In state competition, a 4-H member is limited to six entries, so if he or she has won eight purple ribbons at the county fair, something must be left at home. Even so, there are enough exhibits to pack four auditoriums. Judges begin their work of awarding ribbons: A purple is the top award, followed by blue, red and white. Every 4-H exhibit wins a ribbon.

In one building a dozen or more judges examine the two thousand items of clothing made by 4-H'ers. Everything is turned inside out, this way and that, to check the sleeves and darts and hem and zipper and lining and . . . Each exhibit has a photograph of the 4-H'er wearing the garment, a description of how it fits with the total wardrobe, the cost, the care needed, even the shoes and accessories that go with it. Boys enter clothing, too, in a category called "Young Man Look Right—

Dress Right." This teaches them to choose color and fabric combinations and to plan wardrobes.

In a smaller hall, other judges sit down to tables piled high with cakes, breads, cookies, rolls, muffins and biscuits. Mmmmmm—it smells like a giant cookie jar. The goodies are unwrapped from their plastic bags and sliced and served to each judge. The judges sniff, nibble, savor, poke, compare and comment on two thousand pieces of baked goods. Many are too dry, or sticky, or crumbly, or bitter, or coarse, or tough. And some are just right—in appearance, texture, color and flavor. Those are the purple winners. Once an award is given, a sample goes into an exhibit case. The rest of the item is rewrapped and delivered to the 4-H cafeteria to be served with meals. Lucky diners.

Next to the fresh baked goods are canned foods—over four hundred jars of fruits, vegetables, meats and jellies. One judge is busy turning jars, comparing, holding them to the light, awarding ribbons. The jams and jellies and preserves are tasted, too. All around, the walls are hung with posters about nutrition, another of the 4-H projects.

The horticulture building has several sections—one a sunny room filled with the fresh garden scents of onions and cucumbers and tomatoes and kohlrabi and melons. The judge lines up red cabbages on a table and steps back for a critical look. There are fifteen hundred other vegetables waiting their turn.

This hall holds more than horticulture. One room full of dried grasses and crops has the musty, dusty odor of sorghum

Imagine tasting samples of 2,000 cookies and cakes and breads and rolls. Surplus goes to the cafeteria of the 4-H dormitory.

Home-canned foods get a critical glance from a judge.

heads and newly harvested wheat and oats. A counter display of 4-H scrapbooks shows native grasses and crops, neatly pressed, mounted and labeled.

Another room is chock-full of arts and crafts. Girls and boys have outdone themselves with macrame owls and hanging shelves, hand-tooled belts and billfolds, knitted robes and hats, stuffed animals and pillows. The list is long.

Among the arts and crafts, a pillow display gets last-minute fluffing. Tooled leather belts and purses fill a glass display case. Walls of the exhibit hall are hung with macrame.

The central room of the building is crowded with refinished furniture, polished and gleaming. One corner has a display of terrariums and shelves of insect collections. In each section, judging goes on until late night and begins early the next day.

There are exhibits on electricity and veterinary science and child development. One girl has written a family history, documenting her great-great-grandfather's homesteading in Dakota Territory in 1859; it says that when the area opened for settlement, land sold for $1.25 an acre. Another exhibit hardly needs a "Don't touch" sign—inside the glass case, hundreds of bees swarm over four large honeycombs.

Meander to a fourth 4-H exhibit hall, where a judge is hanging a purple ribbon on a rock collection. "These young rock hounds get better every year," he says proudly. Each specimen is mounted and labeled as to type and place of finding. "And be sure you see the fossils," he adds, pointing to other cases.

Nearby are five hundred photographs 4-H'ers have taken of local subjects and their personal interests: school athletics, the grain harvest, 4-H rodeos, canning peaches, Indian dances, horseshoeing, even an old shed in all stages of burning to the ground.

The exhibits go on and on—and those already mentioned are only the projects entered at the fair by 4-H members. Every boy or girl with a skill, a hobby, or a talent can send an exhibit to the fair—in the "open" classes which are for all ages and all interests. If you can weave a wall hanging, or construct a model airplane, or knit a vest, or bake bread, or cook up apricot jam, or make the best fudge on the block, you'll find competition at the state fair. Stories and poems have special categories, too, and schools from all across the state send art and educational exhibits. Ten-foot-tall display walls are hung with finger paintings and puppets and arithmetic workbooks and origami and posters and maps and oil paintings and papier-mâché and science scrapbooks—all done by students, grades one through twelve. A state fair catalogue describes every competition—in case you have a specialty, or want the entire class to enter.

But you haven't met anyone yet! Come along. The livestock exhibits arrive the day before the fair opens—and so do the boys and girls. . . .

2

"With an oink-oink here . . ."

Trucks and pickups waited in line behind the livestock barns. All day and into the evening 4-H livestock arrived at the fair—all the chickens and the cattle and the pigs and the sheep and the rabbits and . . .

The barns were no longer deserted and quiet. Straw was pitched into each pen as bedding. Animals were fed and watered and led outside for baths. Yes, baths.

Marty Pearson, thirteen years old, got up "with the chickens." He had chores to do, breakfast to eat, sheep and pigs to load and a fair to go to. He didn't want to waste a minute. The straw hat clamped over his dark, curly hair gave him the air of a cowpuncher.

It was a seventy-mile trip to the fair, but by noon his four sheep and two pigs were already unloaded and he had tied one of the sheep to a telephone pole near the barn. Marty held a water hose with one hand and sudsed the sheep's wool with the other. (Wait until his mother looked for her dishwashing soap.) The sheep fidgeted, sidestepped, shook, ducked and finally wedged itself between the pole and a wall, but there was no escaping that bath.

The sheep and swine shared an open-sided barn. There were about 800 sheep and 550 pigs complaining about it, too. In the center of the barn was a large fenced arena where the animals would be shown. Bleachers stretched along one side. The aisles of the sheep section became crowded barbershops, as last-minute clippings groomed the animals for the next day's judging. Tufts of wool speckled the dirt floor and blew about. After clipping, the sheep were "blocked," their wool fluffed with a steel-tined brush, so it was soft and spongy to touch. Market lambs, a category judged for the quality of meat they carry, are close-cropped. The breeding stock are usually left fluffier, with longer fleece, for showing. (The 4-H sheep category is limited to lambs and yearlings.)

Anyone who wasn't at work washing or clipping felt duty bound to sit on top of a pen and offer good advice and helpful directions. But the "helpers" didn't slow Marty down. When he finished his sheep, he had pigs to wash. And places to go and people to meet. That was another thing about the fair—all the new friends. And the competition. And the livestock shows. Ask him if he likes animals and he says "Yeah . . ." But his easy, curling smile says more: He likes them a lot.

"No, I don't get nervous when I show my livestock," he says. "When I was younger I did. I've shown for eight years, since

15

Marty Pearson readies a lamb for competition. "You do get attached to your 4-H livestock," he says; "especially to the ones you bring to the fair. Most kids sell them here and it's kind of hard."

Everyone snacks at the fair, especially if the feed bag just happens to be open. The sheep in the next stall invites himself.

I was five. Before I was in 4-H, I showed sheep in the open classes, where there aren't any age limits. With 4-H I've been here five years. Yup, I really like the fair!"

Marty bunked in the 4-H dorm for fair week, in a big room with twenty-five other boys. "Gets noisy, but it's fun—people tell jokes and stuff. I have a lot of friends up here." Marty's slim figure steamed off to finish his work.

On the other side of the barn Neal Foster was unloading his pigs. At fifteen, Neal moved with quiet assurance, a blond outdoorsman. He headed the animals toward a scale where their weights were recorded. Each pig received an ear tag identification, a combination staple and pierced earring. "My pigs are in the market category, which means they were raised for their meat," says Neal. "They weigh about 260 pounds each, so they're in the heavyweight competition. Lightweight runs from 200 to 220 pounds, and heavyweight is anything over 220.

"My dad raises pigs, and these were born on our farm in February. One's a market gilt and one's a market barrow." (A gilt is a female and a barrow is a castrated boar.)

Neal plans to sell his pigs at the 4-H livestock sale on the final day of the fair. "Last year the meat-packing plant sent me 'cutout data' on my pigs—that tells you the quality of the meat you raised. You want a pig to give a good loin eye. That's the round piece of meat inside the rib—it ought to be a three- to six-inch diameter. What you don't want is lots of back fat—not more than an inch thick. In the show ring, the judge estimates what kind of meat he thinks the pig is carrying."

The swine judging was scheduled for early on opening morn-

Neal Foster wields a stiff brush to groom his pig for competition the next day.

ing, so Neal's first job was grooming his pigs. He herded them to the outdoor pens, carrying along the garden hose he'd brought from home. After wetting them, he rubbed them with a bar of soap and lathered and scrubbed them with a stiff brush. On each side, other 4-H boys and girls sudsed and rinsed. Spectators standing too close were also sudsed and rinsed.

Once the pigs were clean, their skins glowing a vigorous pink, they were returned to their pen. With fresh bedding and luck, they would stay clean until morning. Neal poured out ten pounds of ground oats and corn from the hundred-pound bag he had brought for the week. The pigs didn't wait to be invited.

Neal, a 4-H member for seven years, has always lived on the same farm. "My dad grew up just a half mile from where we live, and my grandparents still live on that farm." His family history makes Neal a traditional farm boy at a time when farm populations are getting smaller.

What is not traditional is that in the morning, when a boy might be expected to race for the barn and chores, Neal is more apt to rush to school for early football practice—at six-thirty or seven o'clock. Fortunately the pigs feed themselves whenever they want—from a self-feeder, a large bin with feed running in automatically. Modern farming is handy for a boy with other things on his mind.

Neal's class at school has about two hundred students. When football season ends, wrestling begins. Teams travel long distances to compete, in these states with lots of space and few people. "We go out to Pierre, and that takes four hours by charter bus," Neal says. "We went there for wrestling this year, and on the way home the bus driver was stopped for speeding. We got home at two in the morning." That trip probably seemed even longer for the driver.

But, what about farm work—the planting and the plowing? "Well, in July," Neal begins, "I went to a wilderness camp in the Bighorn Mountains of Wyoming. And before that there was a church youth meeting for a week in Winnipeg, Manitoba." So much for a typical summer on the farm.

Then Neal adds, "I drove the combine some at harvest. And in June we mowed hay and raked it and baled it and stacked it. Then I detassled seed corn for one of the hybrid corn companies—they pay about $1.90 an hour. And sometimes I bale for neighbors, and that pays about $2.30 an hour.

"A friend, Jeff Hoffelt, and I are giving a safety demonstration here at the fair, and we've practiced that a lot this summer." At the fair Neal stayed with Jeff, whose parents had brought their camper. It was one of a thousand parked in assigned lots around the fairgrounds. Scattered among the campers were tents and, here and there, sleeping bags unrolled under trees. All across the town of Huron, fairgoers crowded in. Lawns and driveways were filled with campers. Every hotel and motel room was booked months in advance. Even private homes rented rooms.

Neal and Jeff had a tent. What they did not have were tent pegs. The tent lay like a deflated raft, while the two admirals discussed the missing pegs. Finally they fastened it with a

Neal Foster, right, and Jeff Hoffelt opt for the outdoor life by raising a tent on the fair campgrounds.

screwdriver, a tire wrench and two sticks. There were better things to do; besides, they wanted to practice their safety demonstration again.

All around the barns, under floodlights, the last livestock to arrive were still being bathed. Hoses sprayed, pigs complained, kids raced. Fair week had begun.

• • •

No one slept late on opening day. Swine judging began at eight o'clock, and chores began even earlier in the beef-cattle barn, the dairy barn, the hog and sheep pens. Neal decided not

21

to feed his pigs before showing them. "They'll look too fat if I do," he explained. Market pigs ought to look as though the carcass has no excess fat.

In the first class of exhibitors there was a familiar face. Marty Pearson earnestly herded his hog to keep it moving, to keep it between himself and the judge, to show it off to best advantage—so the judge could study it front to rear.

Over the loudspeaker one judge viewed the competition: "Some of these pigs are carrying maybe a little more grease than we'd like . . . but at these weights, we'll have to accept some grease on 'em. Some are kind of narrow and kind of shallow and kind of hard growin'. We're also judging for showmanship—forty percent on the grooming of the animal, twenty percent on the dress of the individual showing, and the rest on how they present their animal to the judge."

Marty kept his eyes on the judge and his mind on business. He kept the pig out of the corners and moving. It paid off with two purple ribbons—one for showmanship, one for the animal. Marty gave the pig a pat of congratulations on the way to the pen.

Another class began. Pigs spilled into the arena like broncos loose in a pasture. This was a heavyweight division, and Neal came in, scrambling to recapture his pig. He carried a heavy crooked stick to herd the animal. Pigs can be stubborn. Some would rather root in the dirt floor of the arena than stroll around. Often it takes a nudge with the cane, a slap on the rump, or one swift kick to keep pigs moving. Other times they

22

Thirty pigs in the ring make a lively competition. "We just stay with them," says Neal Foster, center. "It's hard to make a hog stand still."

are downright unsociable and fight. When that happens, ring attendants rush up carrying plywood screens to thrust between the pigs to separate them. Once diverted, the pigs either amble away or turn and bite the next handy porker.

Judges walked inside the arena, considering the livestock. Occasionally they would signal for a pig to be moved into a side pen, either a blue ribbon pen or a red ribbon one. Those left in the center were purple ribbon winners. Neal's first pig was still in the ring, and Neal happily accepted a purple ribbon, shoving it in a rear pocket while he guided the pig back to its

23

own pen. Although it was already eleven o'clock, his second pig would not be shown until later.

Other 4-H areas were stirring on opening morning. In the horticulture building another Jeff, Jeff Moser, gathered his props for a ten-minute talk on entomology. And at the dairy barn Jodi Liebnow groomed Rosie, her dairy heifer, for competition in the dairy show next day. It would be nine-year-old Jodi's first state fair as a 4-H exhibitor.

By lunchtime 4-H'ers and spectators alike were hungry. But what to choose? Maybe ribs roasted over charcoal . . . and homemade apple pie . . . and fresh lemonade. They could eat and listen to a free rock concert at the band shell. Then it would be time to race to another 4-H competition, such as the photo judging, which Neal had entered.

This competition, like all judging events, tested a 4-H'er's knowledge of a field, in this case photography. Neal and a hundred others in the senior division (fourteen years and over) examined a group of photographs for quality, composition, originality and other checkpoints. They answered questions such as "Which picture has the best use of focus?" "Which has the worst background?" Knowing what makes some photos better than others helps a 4-H'er train his eye for his own photography.

Neal was due at the second swine competition at the same time. He zipped through the photos in seven and a half minutes and set out at a lope for the arena. He arrived as his class was almost over. Jeff had shown Neal's hog, which had received a blue ribbon. "He was one of the last ones sent to the blue pen," Jeff said. "There were only two purple." Three competitions were over for Neal—with the safety talk still to come. He and Jeff went off to practice it "one last time." It needed to be just right for the State Fair.

While they were practicing, another boy in another town, John Wheeting, looked away from his math assignment. Three days until the weekend. Three days until he could go to the fair. Many schools opened before the fair and hundreds of students counted the days like John.

Meanwhile, it's almost suppertime at the fair. How about a steaming bowl of chili? At one food stand a waitress was saying, "He offered me four free rides if I'd give him my earrings, but I mean, they're my best, they're turquoise." People with jackets and pillows streamed past on their way to the grandstand show starring Johnny Cash. Jodi Liebnow said good night to Rosie the heifer and went off to the grandstand, too, but she was so tired she almost slept through the show.

In the 4-H arena another livestock judging had begun at six o'clock. This time it was sheep, and there was Marty again, kneeling to get a firm hold on his animal. Eighty-five sheep in a ring, even washed-sudsed-rinsed-clipped-trimmed-and-blocked beauties, make a racket. Each girl and boy holds their lamb—they do not herd them as in the swine division. The judges pace through the rows, eyeing the animals from all angles, sending this one to the red or blue line and that one to the purple. The bleachers are filled

There is a good deal of snipping, brushing and fussing the day before the 4-H sheep competition. Some groom their sheep on platforms which have neck rings to hold the animal—others favor this between-the-knees grip.

with families, watching intently, slipping down to snap pictures.

One lamb objected strenuously to the whole show and made a sudden lunge for freedom. The small boy in charge grabbed for it. Missed. Raced after it and threw himself in a full-length tackle. He caught only the hind heels and was dragged several inches. The lamb bolted free. On all sides a flurry of bleating rose. Two judges helped corral the animal, and the grim-faced boy led it back in place.

Marty and his lamb were serenely quiet. After eight years of showing, not much worries Marty. "I'd rather show sheep than pigs," he says, "sheep are about my favorites to raise, although lately, I'm kind of liking the little pigs, too."

When the class ended Marty had both the showmanship purple ribbon and the award for top lamb in the group of eighty-five. "This is the lamb I'm going to take to the Ak-Sar-Ben in Omaha," he says proudly. "It's the largest 4-H livestock show in the world." Marty showed there when he was twelve and earned a seventh-place showmanship award, while his lamb got a blue ribbon. The idea of entering Ak-Sar-Ben was his brother's, but the effort and determination were all Marty's. (Ak-Sar-Ben . . . a strange name for a show? Spell Nebraska backward and see what you get.)

Marty also had his sights set on buying more lambs with his 4-H earnings—either from a farmer who breeds livestock, or at an auction sale. Members of 4-H are encouraged to keep records: initial price of the livestock, feed costs, sale price and profit. Most earnings come through livestock projects, but a 4-H'er with garden produce from a horticulture project, or one with twenty acres of oats, might sell the surplus crop and bank a profit. Even arts and crafts can fatten a wallet.

Marty already had about fifteen ewes, seven hogs and two cattle. And one of a special new breed—a Kawasaki 125.

"I got the motorcycle myself," says Marty. "I got it from pigs and sheep—from selling them. Took more than one year's work. It cost eight hundred forty dollars. I usually just buy livestock. For the motorcycle I needed my folks' approval, but for sheep and animals they don't say much. They let me use my judgment. This year, though, first thing is to pay my feed bill. When you're younger, the feed store will let you wait until you sell your livestock to pay: I've got a five-hundred-dollar feed bill." He planned to sell his pigs at the 4-H livestock sale at the State Fair.

"Some of my pigs are awful big, and the buyers will cut 'em down for being so big—'cause their meat gets tougher. But I would say, hopefully, they'll bring about forty-seven cents a pound."

Before showing his swine, unlike Neal, Marty fed them. "Some people don't. I do because they're shown at nine o'clock, and they're used to being fed at seven-thirty and they get gaunt. But with sheep, it's a lot harder. When you feed them hay they get potbellied and that makes them look shorter. So I fed them this morning, but not hay . . . well, hardly enough to measure."

"Marty's the best little choreboy," says his mother, "but

when the lambs arrive we have to fight to keep him from going out to the barn to check on them every night. Doesn't matter if it's icy and snowy, out he goes in the middle of the night."

Marty grins. "I usually get out. After all, the ewes could get hurt lambing and the flies could get on them. Lots of things. It's good to check."

His morning chores must be done by seven-thirty, when the school bus arrives to take him the seventeen miles to school. He'd have his eighth-grade work to catch up on after the fair, but that was fine with him—the social studies would be fun. And there would be basketball to look forward to—and track (running the hundred and the two-twenty and the hurdles). And his motorcycle to ride. And the trip to Omaha!

"I want to go to school, to college," Marty says eagerly, "but I'm sure I'm going to be a farmer. I'd never . . . I don't know how I could live in a city . . . even a small city. I just like watching them on television, but not to live there."

In the show ring he deftly won another purple ribbon. He had collected his first ribbon at nine o'clock that morning and was still at it by nine in the evening. He exhibited six animals in a single day and had one blue and five purple ribbons to show for it.

Neal and Jeff ambled by and stopped to watch a few minutes of the sheep show on their way to the midway—to do "nothin'." They didn't bother to check Neal's pigs; but a glance in their pen shows them nestled in the yellow straw, sleeping blissfully.

3

"Can she bake a cherry pie?"

Shelly McFarland, age eleven, crawled down from her top bunk in the girls' dorm at six o'clock the second morning of the fair. She had been awake nearly an hour, battling the butterflies in her stomach. Her rosy cheeks felt stiff, and she could barely muster a smile, let alone her bubbly laugh. This was the morning of the junior special-foods competition.

She hoped she had everything she needed. She hoped the judge wouldn't ask her a question she couldn't answer. She hoped . . . "I got to the State Fair," she told herself, "at least I accomplished that, whatever ribbon I get today. . . . But it's nice getting a good one." Shelly dressed in a blue jumper with flowers embroidered on its bib. The color matched her lively blue eyes. She had made the dress herself and entered it in the county fair. It made her feel good—if only those butterflies would get lost.

Shelly choked down a little breakfast and sighed a lot, trying to relax. She checked through her big carton of supplies again. She was scheduled in the first group of cooks, which meant that at seven-thirty in the morning she entered the kitchens of the local high school to concoct her special dish for a panel of judges. Each shift would last an hour and a half. There were twenty-one girls waiting and fidgeting. This junior competition (for those thirteen years and under) would continue until three o'clock that day, five shifts in all, a total of ninety-five girls and two boys.

The home-economics kitchens of the local high school are bustling. Each shift has twenty-one cooks, everyone preparing a favorite recipe. One boy served up a dish he called "Rhubarb Pizza."

The young cooks were to fully prepare a dish from one of the four basic food groups: milk, meat, bread-cereal, vegetable-fruit. They had to suggest a one-meal menu that included their specialty and to know the cost for each serving of it.

Each competitor was assigned a kitchen work area. Shelly taped a brown paper bag to the edge of the counter for scraps. She arranged the ingredients for her specialty—Hamburger Delight. Once she started slicing the onions and green peppers and browning the hamburger, she seemed calmer, sure of her work. Shelly used an electric skillet, although others used the stove tops and ovens as they needed. Here and there bells chimed to say something was ready. The smell of tomato sauce and curry and meatballs and biscuits drifted through the room. No one talked; they were much too busy. One girl knelt as she ladled crushed ice into an ice cream freezer.

As the cooks worked, judges moved about the kitchens, watching and asking them questions about nutrition—another area of this 4-H project. By 8:15 most of the dishes were in the oven, or simmering, or cooling—depending on what they required. Each cook neatly cleared away utensils and wiped the counter clean for the next person.

As soon as Shelly's food was simmering in the skillet she hurried into the hall to arrange a table setting, a part of the competition. Shelly had packed her china in newspaper and now she unwrapped it and set it out just so. Each place setting included a centerpiece: One had a model covered wagon with a small corn-husk doll.

32

When the food was ready, the competitors waited their turn before the "tasting" judges. Some girls paced nervously, peeking into the judging room. One blew on burned fingers. One would admit to the judges, "I really don't like this broccoli, but my little brother does."

Shelly was the first to present her dish, decorated with wedges of cheese and circles of green pepper. She smiled and spoke in a clear voice. "My family likes it. It's quick and easy. And the tomatoes and peppers are from our garden, so it's in season now. We always have hamburger and tomato sauce on hand. You could leave out the fancies on this dish, but for show I thought it would be best."

A judge asked what vitamins it contained. "B_2 and C and A in the tomatoes and green pepper," said Shelly. "It cost between fifty and seventy-five cents a serving." Then the judges asked for a taste and Shelly cut slices; but not deep enough, and the serving slipped from the ladle. "Oooooh," she said, "I didn't get it cut far enough." She quickly scooped up a second slice.

After the questions, Shelly placed the dish beside her place setting. "Am I glad it's done!" she said. "Sometimes I wonder why I go through all this, but once it's over I'm glad I did."

"Most of the junior group cook from established recipes," said a judge. "In the senior group, the fourteen-and-overs, some use original recipes, but not the juniors."

That judge had reckoned without Shelly. "I saw my dish in a magazine," she said, "and I thought, boy this looks pretty.

Shelly McFarland is quiet but hopeful as she meets the "tasting judges." Questions and tasting last between five and ten minutes.

Shelly spoons "Hamburger Delight" onto layers of French bread, which she slices lengthwise. "It's sort of hard to get it level all the way through," she says.

Shelly's blue ribbon winner is as tasty as it looks, decorated with cheese, green peppers and tomato slices.

It's going to be nice for a contest. So I took that picture and looked at it really hard and figured out what was in it. I made up my own spices—you know I really couldn't tell how that meat tasted, but it worked out. It has onions, salt, pepper, Worcestershire sauce, hamburger and Spanish-style tomato sauce. We have to take the labels off cans before the competition, that's the only restriction. You can't have brands or advertising."

Shelly's home is at the northern tip of the Black Hills. She travels three miles into town for school, a sixth-grade class of fifteen students. "We live in a valley, and if we drive about a mile, we can see Bear Butte. We see lots of deer and we tend to see quite a few snakes. There's lots of irrigation, and they just love that swampy ground. I'm not used to them and I'm scared to death!"

Besides her cooking, Shelly planned to participate in the dairy-judging competition. She would not show an animal, but practice judging—using her knowledge to select the top animal of a group. Her choice and the reasons for it would earn a ribbon.

"Dairy is my favorite area," she said. "My folks had a dairy farm, and I've milked cows and everything. And my calf . . . oh, Elizabeth is really special to me. Some kids, they jerk their calves around, but this is my only calf, and I take care of her. Next year she'll have a calf and I'll show it."

This was Shelly's third year in 4-H. Another year she also hoped to show her horse. "It's a beautiful bay with black legs.

When it was little it was really nervous, and I was the one who halterbroke it, and so it became mine. I've worked with animals since I was very young. To halterbreak, first we'd have to rope the colt, and it'd struggle and be ornery. That's a good way for a colt to learn not to do it. Then you put the halter on and leave it on for about two weeks. And then you put the lead strap on and you pull them around. You have to be really *careful*, because colts tend to jump up and you could get under one. They're little things, but they could hurt you awfully bad. This colt was the shyest one and it got so it would follow me.

"My colt's named Depression and his older brother is named Drought. It's just the opposite of my colt, gentle and fairly well broken. My colt is still scared of things. We have horses named Disaster and Desperation, too. A show horse needs a colorful name."

Besides her calf and colt and cooking, Shelly helps with other farm work. "We don't have as many chores now as we did with the dairy," she says, "but I can plow and disk and drive the tractor. I'd like some more chores. I'd like some lambs." Her vegetable garden produced blue ribbon beets and beans at the county fair. And she makes some of her own school clothing—she has for three years.

"Yip, I'm going to college," she says in her positive, sprightly way, "and I'm going to teach . . . the really small ones—kindergarten." She plans to earn some of her college money. "And I hope I'll get a scholarship, because I know it'll take a lot of money to go to college."

If you sit anywhere long enough, especially at a state fair, someone you know will come by. For instance: Marty stalked through the 4-H dining hall. He looked annoyed. "I just found out I have a staph infection in my finger, and I have to take time to go to a doctor," he said. "Last year I had one on this hand. And then there's a rumor about swine dysentery in the barn, and if that's true every pig in the state can get it. It's very contagious—just walk through an infected puddle and you carry it home with you." He shook his head over these new worries and went out to check his livestock.

Shelly wanted to visit other 4-H exhibits, now that her cooking stint was finished. In arts and crafts she liked a plastic molded chess set, although "I play more checkers than chess." She was delighted with the purple ribbon on her sister's project in child development.

"My sister made this dress for the little girl we baby-sit," Shelly explained. "It had to be a learning thing—so the pockets have appliqués of L and R for *left* and *right*, and it has a zipper and red buttons, and it has 'out-stitching' that has to be really straight. Oh, I understand why she got a purple."

Finally Shelly stopped to listen to a high school band in a free concert. One of the drummers was another 4-H member with his own projects at the State Fair. Like Shelly, Jeff Moser had butterflies—but not in his stomach; his were under glass.

Jeff, sandy-haired, tall and slim at fifteen, gave an entomology talk titled "What Bugs You?" To illustrate his speech he brought a case of twenty-five specimens, butterflies and moths,

37

part of his collection of over a hundred mounted insects. For the program Jeff wore a nifty patterned shirt—he looked more city slicker than cowboy, although his summer chores included feeding ninety-eight calves each day.

During the fair, 4-H members presented a total of 430 talks, or demonstrations, on many topics, anything from grooming animals to citizenship to sewing buttonholes. Sample the titles: "The Case of the Murdered Molar," "In a Pig's Ear," "To Knot or Not to Knot," "Everything You Always Wanted to Know About Eggs, but Were Too Chicken to Ask."

Talks went on in four locations, every day and all day. Speakers were judged on their knowledge, organization, poise, clarity and visual aids. The audience usually included speakers waiting to go on, parents and a few county agents. Every speaker could count on the judge to ask a question after a talk— like a quickie quiz.

Before his talk Jeff "borrowed" his exhibit case from the entomology entries. Another case in the exhibit had a familiar name—Neal Foster. Neal had already checked on his entry. "Those insects," he complained. "You have to be so careful. They're apt to go to pieces on you at the last minute . . . just as you try to pin them. They fall apart."

Jeff Moser could sympathize, after five years of entomology projects. "If you just jiggle them they'll break. Takes a lot of time and being careful."

If Jeff was nervous, it didn't show during his talk. He had drawn large charts of insects and painted them in colors bright enough to stand out in the small room. He spoke with authority, holding up his twenty-five-insect exhibit and showing another one which held a large mounted cecropia moth. In bottles on the table before him were examples of early stages of the moth's development, each preserved in formaldehyde, each collected by Jeff.

"I couldn't bring the whole collection," Jeff said later. "This box of twenty-five was collected from May to July of this summer. Whenever we turn on the sprinkler in the vegetable garden it draws all sorts of moths and butterflies.

"That big cecropia moth, I found one Sunday morning," he said. "I went out to do chores and I saw this moth by the gas tank. So I ran back to the house—I've got jars all over the place for an emergency like this, it drives Mom crazy—and I grabbed a big jar that wouldn't damage the wings. I think he had just hatched and was drying his wings, so I didn't need a net. He was on grass, and I cut the grass and just slid it all into the jar.

"With a moth I usually use formaldehyde on cotton—put it under their mouth, proboscis, whatever. But *once*, that big cecropia . . . I had him mounted for a month and he revived. He was alive! He is quite large and strong, and evidently the formaldehyde wasn't potent enough. So . . . well, I don't think he'll come alive again."

With flies and small insects like bees, Jeff does not use a chemical in his "kill jar," but simply caps the jar until the insect dies. "You can't leave the lid on after a day, though," he said, "because the bug becomes hard and you might as well not have caught him. Throw it away, because you can't manage the wings. I wouldn't kill a moth by suffocation, because they become restless and flap around and might damage their wings. They'd lose a lot of their wing scales."

Some of Jeff's bug collection has come about through another interest of his—rock and fossil collecting. "When you pick up a rock, you can find a lot of things," he said, laughing, ". . . mostly ants—but sometimes an interesting bug."

His rock and fossil exhibit was in another building on the fairgrounds, hung with a purple ribbon. Most of the rocks and fossils were collected in his home county. "Being farmers we've got to clear the land and pick rocks, and lots of times I find an interesting one and set it up by Dad on the tractor."

Jeff's been collecting rocks for four years, which means boxes of specimens—next to the dozens of kill bottles—all over the house.

"We live two miles from a park, the Rose Hill Park, and I find lots of fossils there. There's a man-made dam, and when it was built they discovered a layer of adobe houses from the Arikara Indians. There was evidence of their huts and other artifacts. And at the dam and around the road which they built, dozens of arrowheads turned up. Also there's an Indian burial ground in our neighbor's pasture, and a creek runs through it and onto our land, and I find arrowheads along the banks.

"This is probably my favorite fossil." He pointed to an inch-thick rock with the print of a fern showing. "When you turn this rock over, there's another fern print on the other side!"

40

Jeff Moser wins a purple ribbon, top award, for his fossil exhibit. Exhibitors are limited to six entries, so Jeff had to leave a favorite arrowhead collection at home. Club members may, however, compete in speaking and judging events in addition to their six entries.

Jeff has learned rock identification through his own reading—books he's collected or checked out of the library—just as he learned about entomology. "But if I really get stumped on identifying a rock or fossil, I can send it to one of the state universities and get help."

Jeff lives twenty-five miles from school, where he joins in

speech and debate, the yearbook and school newspaper and the chorus. And football. "Well, I try to play end or tackle, but sometimes I play the bench position."

For the first eight grades Jeff attended a country school— and was the only one in his class. Entering high school he had to enroll in a larger school. "It's nice," he says of his new school. "It's a lot of kids. Our class is about a hundred ten. With so many, they give you one assignment and you work on it and that's all. In a country school, when you were done with one thing you went right to another. I think you get more work and education in a country school. In the time I was in country school, the first year there were six altogether in the school and over the years it went up to twenty-two, down to thirteen, and the last year I was there, there were eight."

Jeff and his family have traveled through most of the western states. "I don't like the cities," he said, "too noisy and too crowded." He likes reading—"when I'm sick and there's nothing else to do." Cooking—"anything with a recipe." With all his interests he hasn't decided yet about college. "I'm not sure what I want." Meanwhile, he isn't "bugged" about it.

• • •

Jeff's entomology exhibit went back on display. Next to the entomology area were shelves filled with terrariums—mini-gardens, perhaps. The terrariums came in all shapes and sizes: bottles, jars, enormous snifters, fish tanks—anything. Two youngsters had made their own glass containers. One in the shape of a house was twenty inches by twelve inches, fastened with lead strips at the seams. The peaked roof lifted free for easy gardening. Another large terrarium had a smaller fish bowl in the center, with a goldfish swimming there.

"The overall design is most important," said the terrarium judge. "Youngsters ought to plan before they plant, try things this way and that before actually setting them in. Plants need to have good scale, and variety and balance. They shouldn't be overcrowded either. Design is the first thing we look for—it should be pleasing to the eye."

The judge studied the rows of terrariums. "The glass makes a difference, too. Some glass is not easy to see through—personally I think the colored glass terrariums are difficult to view. But whatever the glass, boys and girls who have home terrariums ought to be careful to keep them clean and shining—both because it looks pretty and because it keeps the plants healthier.

"Another area I criticize, as a judge, is a poor mixture of plants. For example, cactus should never be placed in a terrarium with moisture-loving plants—like ferns. The combinations should be plants which might grow naturally together. Cactus is best reserved for open dish gardens. Terrariums are great fun as projects or hobbies. There are lots of books to help a youngster start one, and everyone enjoys watching them grow."

4

"Thought I heard a chicken sneeze . . ."

One building on the fairgrounds echoed like a schoolyard at recess. There was a rooster "saying his prayers" and another one "singing a hymn to the hens upstairs." And beyond came a crow . . . a cackle . . . a cluck . . . a puck-puck-pucket . . . and a screech. Wire cages stacked on wire cages filled the poultry barn. Aisles were only wide enough to squeeze through, so close the hens muttered threats as you passed.

The superintendent of the poultry exhibits lifted a small chicken from its cage. "This is a white Cochin bantam," he explained. "It's six months old and full size. It weighs about twenty or twenty-four ounces. They're ornamental birds and when they're raised from chicks they make good pets. This one has been bathed and is ready to show."

Even the chickens get baths! Use dishwashing detergent, warm water and great care—plus gentle drying under a heat

There's more to chickens than laying eggs—this one exhibits fancy feathers. Poultry competition is open to everyone—farmers, hobbyists, 4-H members and other boys and girls.

lamp, so the feathers become fluffy and the bird doesn't risk catching cold and really sneezing. Judging is based on breed characteristics and show preparations, such as cleanliness. The bantam strutted proudly, placing her wide, feathered feet as precisely as a high-wire artist.

"Even a person with a small yard could consider raising these birds," said the superintendent. "They're available at commercial pet-supply companies and through breeders who exhibit at fairs. Any boy or girl with a favorite bird could enter it in their state fair." All fairs have entry blanks and booklets describing requirements and entry fees. The cost for entering the bantam was fifty cents.

After the chickens' uproar, the pigeons were cooing peaceably. They carried fancy names, like dragoons and fantails and frill backs and damascenes. Some were pure white and others a pearl gray edged with pink and green. But even their cooing was a racket compared to the rabbits in stacked cages at the far end of the building.

Two purple ribbons, fluttering on the pens of a copper and a red satin rabbit, delighted nine-year-old Jodi Liebnow. They were her rabbits. Her face lost its shyness as she leaned forward and beamed a smile at them. Her dark eyes checked the water bowls out of habit. On her parents' dairy farm, a few miles from the fairgrounds, it is Jodi's responsibility to water the family's 150 rabbits. The job takes her an hour each morning—and again each evening. One coop of twenty-five rabbits is totally in her care. She must feed them as well as water them.

Jodi pulled a bag of sunflower seeds from the pocket of her checkered pants and munched as she visited her rabbits. This was Jodi's first year in 4-H work—and her first week as a third grader. "Not today though," she said with an impish smile; "we sort of skipped." Purple ribbons can be mighty tempting.

"At county achievement day we had to hold our own rabbits, or put them on a little counter," Jodi explained, "and then the judge came by. Before you show them you always put some

46

Jodi Liebnow cradles her rabbit gently but firmly, so it won't become frightened and struggle. Most of the rabbits on her parents' farm are large varieties grown for their meat. Rabbits cared for by Jodi earned six purple ribbons at the State Fair.

water on your hand and rub it over them to get all the loose hair off."

"The rabbits here at the fair," said the exhibit judge, "are two classes: meat and show. The meat rabbits grow to about ten to twelve pounds and may also be in a show. But smaller rabbits, like the American Dutch and English Spot, mature at four to five pounds and are only show. Show is judged mostly for uniform color; the meat class for amount and quality, which we judge by the feel of the animal."

Many rabbit owners and judges bear marks of their work—long scratches on their forearms. "The rabbits don't hurt intentionally," said the judge, "but they have a certain amount of fear, and some breeds have awful sharp toenails and, of course, strong hind legs. However, an animal that is raised with a child is a safe pet."

Jodi added, "You have to pick them up careful, holding behind the neck and under the rump. But *never* by their ears."

Besides the small breeds, there are dwarf varieties of all breeds which make good pets for homes or apartments. The judge said, "This fair has 170 rabbit entries and is open to anyone—no age restrictions, no state boundaries. Anyone in the world can enter a rabbit here."

At the fair Jodi's rabbits needed little of her attention, but she had another entry which got tender loving care. That was her Holstein dairy heifer Rosie. (A heifer is a cow that hasn't yet borne a calf.) It was about time for Rosie's bath, and Jodi thought she'd better get over to the dairy barn.

"Have you seen the animal nursery?" Jodi asked on the way. "It's in that building. There's puppies and kittens and baby chicks—all to give away. And there's baby ducks and ferrets and ponies to look at." All around the fairgrounds, youngsters

48

carried adopted pups, or tugged them along on rope leashes. The puppy pen was a rough-and-tumble spot, full of high spirits, and a lot of head scratching was needed to choose just one.

Jodi led Rosie out of the barn and tied her near the water faucets. She hooked up the hose with its sprayer-brush attachment, and the bath began. Rosie bawled an unladylike comment, but Jodi kept after her, sudsing, scrubbing and rinsing. She washed Rosie's back and belly and tail and hooves. She dampened a cloth to clean Rosie's ears. "They'll be looking at her eyes to see if they're clear," she explained as she worked, "and at her nose to see if it's clean, and they just look in her ears to see if they're clean. When they judge they look at the front sections; and at the back, which is supposed to be straight; and at the hooks and pins—they should show a little bit [they are the skeletal structure at the rump]; and they look at the legs. When you show, you keep an eye on the judge and keep the calf between you and the judge; and you have to keep her moving."

Jodi picked up a brush and began working at Rosie's tail, getting rid of tangles and making it fluffy. When the bath was finished Jodi tied Rosie in the sunshine to dry. She tied her to a pole with a printed sign: "Please Save Water." Then Jodi ran into the barn to get a pan of feed. When she came back, Rosie was eating the sign.

Shelly had told a story about showing dairy cattle: "It's very unusual—no other livestock are shown backwards but dairy. The calf doesn't go backwards, but you do. You're facing the

Everyone gets wet at bathtime. Jodi cleans Rosie's face with a hose-sprayer. After scrubbing, she combs and fluffs Rosie's tail.

Jodi and Rosie move to the arena for the Holstein heifer calf class. Rosie's coat was rubbed with oil to make it shine and lie flat. A 4-H'er spends weeks working with a calf, leading it so it will work well in the ring at competition time.

cow and leading it while you go backwards. It's very unusual to walk that way. Once at the county fair it was even worse, because the calf stepped on my pants leg and I fell over!"

Would that worry Jodi? "No," she said thoughtfully, "not if I watch where I'm going." She gave Rosie a pan of ground feed, oats and corn, and calf manna, a vitamin supplement. Then Jodi brushed her coat to make it lie smooth.

The next day, before the dairy competition, Rosie had another bath and drying and brushing. And her coat was rubbed with oil to make it shine. Rosie looked fine.

Jodi, however, was tense. After all, leading a six-hundred-pound heifer is not like hauling the family dog around on a leash, or even a rabbit. She fixed the leather show halter on Rosie and smoothed down her own white shirt and pants. White outfits are traditional for showing dairy cattle. Jodi was the youngest entrant in her group of about twenty. She led Rosie from the barn to the ring and took her place in line. There wasn't the trace of a smile on her face. The day before she had said, "If Rosie jumps around, I have to stop her." Maybe she was thinking of that now.

On the fence at one end of the arena, Marty settled down to watch the competition. Although he wasn't entered, a good friend was, and Marty had come to cheer him on.

One cow balked at moving into the ring, so the girl coming up behind grabbed its tail like a crank and gave a twist. The cow moved on. In the ring the 4-H'ers tried to get their animals to stand in a certain position, a procedure known as "setting

Most 4-H'ers carry sticks to help "set up" the cattle; that is, to place the feet properly to show the animal to best advantage. They tote combs or brushes in hip pockets for in-the-ring grooming.

Pacing carefully backward, 4-H'ers keep an eye on the judge as they lead their dairy animals past his scrutinizing eye.

them up." The front legs should be parallel, while in the rear, one leg is slightly ahead of the other. Sometimes the boy or girl carries a pointed stick into the show ring. If the cow stops off position, its owner presses the stick against one of the feet to get the animal to move it back. Often the cow not only moves the foot, but takes an extra step—which brings it all out of line again. Or, the cow obligingly lifts the foot and puts it down in exactly the same spot. The cow is willing to do this five or six times, until the 4-H'er gives up in disgust.

At last the judges had considered, pondered and inspected the cattle and awarded the ribbons. When Jodi and Rosie filed out of the ring, Jodi had a bright red ribbon and a happy smile.

"Did you see what Rosie did?" she demanded. "She just went pluff. She laid right down . . . she just went pluff . . . and I had to get her up again." She led Rosie back to the barn and her stall where Rosie went "pluff" again. This time Jodi thought it fine to stretch out in the hay beside her calf. Her first state competition was over. It would never be as difficult again. Out came a bag of sunflower seeds—time to celebrate.

High time, too, for a visit to the midway and a few of Jodi's favorite rides. What would you expect a shy, soft-spoken girl to choose? The highest ride and the fastest one?

"That one," said Jodi pointing to the Sky Wheel, a giant double Ferris wheel with two spinning wheels on a long revolving arm. It stood six stories tall. "You can see all over the fairgrounds from it. And I like that one. . . ." She waved toward the centrifugal force ride, which spins so fast it pins riders against the side walls. "You can't walk, or move!" Jodi claimed. And you can't. What about the merry-go-round? "Too young."

• • •

Judging beef cattle began on the day named "4-H Day" during fair week. In the beef barns, grooming was in full swing by seven that morning. The animals had been bathed the day before, but now were "blown" with vacuums to fluff their coats and whisk them free of dust and bits of hay. Heavy beef cattle, standing patiently in metal cribs, seemed smug at all the attention.

Tails are combed and brushed to make them fluffy. Some-

Once the stall has been cleaned and the stock fed and watered, a stretch and a rest are in order.

times the fringe is even "teased" like a fancy hairdo, then wound into a ball and fastened. To help hold the shape, the fringe gets a good whiff of hair spray. The reason for shaping the tails is to call attention to the hindquarters of the animals and to make them seem heftier.

Of course, it's not every day that the scent of hair spray wafts among the hay and oats—this all-out grooming is for show. At home most 4-H'ers keep their animals clean, but not pampered. They were keeping the fair barns reasonably tidy, too. One large sign read: "Put manure on south side only."

Besides the beef judging, 4-H members were still participating in other competitions, such as judging foods and nutrition, judging crops and demonstrations. Speaking of demonstrations, it was time for Neal Foster and Jeff Hoffelt to give their talk, "Snap Decisions." Their subject: broken bones.

Earlier in the day they had given the talk at a safety clinic, but that hadn't calmed their nerves. "We've practiced this for hours," Neal repeated as if to convince himself. While they waited, a girl talked about campfire cooking, and another girl made bound buttonholes. When she'd finished there were six buttonholes in need of a coat.

Finally it was Neal and Jeff's turn. They hauled a long table onto the platform stage. Neal opened the talk: "Fifty thousand persons in this state live fifty miles from a doctor's aid. It makes emergency first aid important, especially in the event of broken bones."

At this point Jeff stretched full-length on the table, so Neal

55

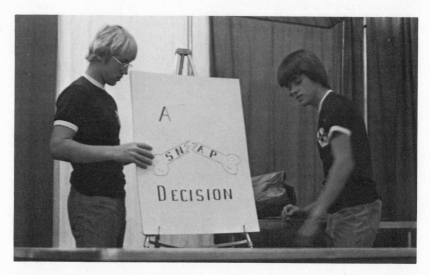

Neal Foster, left, and Jeff Hoffelt set the stage for their safety demonstration on first aid for broken bones.

could demonstrate how to apply an emergency splint for a broken leg. "You'd use materials at hand," he said, "like this steel fence post if it happened in a field." Using strips of torn material and Jeff's belt, he bound the leg to the slim post.

When Neal finished, Jeff untied himself and leaped up—a remarkable recovery. It was his turn to demonstrate, showing proper care for a broken arm, and Neal soon looked like a rodeo reject. From start to finish, their program lasted twenty minutes.

"We never did so poorly," moaned Jeff, who seemed to have fractured his optimism. Neal managed a grin now that it was over. Maybe they'd wander over to the midway again, or to the pinball gallery—a dimly lighted hall where it was easy to lose a few quarters.

Outside the 4-H exhibit building there was the mouth-watering scent of beef roasting over charcoal. In front of the dormitory, concrete blocks outlined two open barbecue pits, each forty feet long. Some twenty-six hundred pounds of beef roast were slowly cooking on the grills. Vats of baked beans simmered. Cartons of potato chips stood open, waiting. By late afternoon, everything was ready for the free 4-H barbecue for members and their families. Six thousand people put away quantities of juicy roast beef sandwiches and ice cream desserts. They sat wherever they found space—under a shady tree, on the tongue of a hay wagon, even on the cement curb.

Jodi came with her family. "And then we went on rides on the midway," she said later, "and my stomach didn't feel so good."

Shelly was there, too, and after the barbecue she went to the evening rodeo. She settled in the large grandstand to watch the opening ceremonies, as a drill team on horseback recreated parade maneuvers of the Seventh Cavalry, which was stationed in the Black Hills in the 1870s.

Then came the first event: a chuck wagon race. There were four wagons drawn by four-horse teams. Besides the driver, each wagon had two "outriders" on horseback. The race recreates roundup days, when the chuck wagon had to break camp in the morning and move on ahead to set up a new camp for evening. With water scarce it was sometimes a dash for the best campsite if several trail herds were moving in the same direction.

At the sound of a gun, the race was on. One outrider dismounted and ran to load a large box (camp gear) onto the rear of the wagon. The wagons and the second riders dashed to the center of the arena, making a circle-eight around designated barrels, and then headed out onto the racetrack. The first outrider followed as soon as he remounted. The arena was a swirl of spinning wheels and straining horses and dust. The crowd cheered. One wagon lost a rear wheel. Another tipped a barrel as it circled, and the barrel bounced beneath the wagon and caught there, bounding ahead of the rear wheels. The wagons and outriders circled a racetrack beyond the arena. The first complete team—wagon and riders—to make the circuit and return to the arena was the winner. The crowd leaped up, craning to see, yelling and clapping.

Rodeos began in America, began with the fall roundup and a gathering of cowboys, a celebration on horseback. Prescott, Arizona, claims the first rodeo was held there on July 4, 1888. But there are records of roping and bronco-riding contests as early as 1847, when ranch hands got together for off-hours betting and competition.

Rodeos have changed over the years. Introducing the cowboys, today's announcer is apt to talk of where they attended college. Or to speak of a horse "psyching" a cowboy, or the "apogee" of the bull's bucking. Which brings the rodeo neatly into the space age.

Some 4-H competitions are part rodeo. This is a "calf scramble" at the Fryeburg Fair in Maine. (Maine Department of Agriculture Photo)

On the other hand, the announcer still tells the rodeo clown: "Rush right over there, George, and grab that bull by the tail. You'll get a real kick out of it." Or, "How do you spell *farm*, George?" And the clown says, *"E-I-E-I-O."*

Rodeo clowns are fast on their feet. They have to be—it's their job to divert the bull's attention once he's shucked the cowboy into the dust. Shelly watched them carefully. "My uncle is a rodeo clown in Texas," she said, "and about a month ago he wasn't so fast. He got his leg broken, and now he's out of a job."

The fair rodeo was an R.C.A.-sanctioned event, meaning all the riders were members of the Rodeo Cowboys Association. "These R.C.A. rodeos," said Shelly, "they're too professional. I really like the kind we have in small towns like New Underwood, or even in our neighbor's corral, 'cause you never know what might happen there. They're exciting."

Still she clapped and laughed at the antics of the clown and oohed when the riders came out pitching on the back of a bull.

"Hang on there, Ed," said the announcer. But at one point the score was Bulls 4, Cowboys 0.

And when the last calf had been roped and the last chuck wagon had raced and the last bull had been coaxed out of the arena, there were bright, shooting fireworks against the night sky.

The barbecue pits had been dismantled in front of the 4-H dormitory. In their place was a platform, where two teens played rock tapes under a floodlight. Other teens danced on the lawn in the circle of light and around the shadowy edges. Nearby, a few boys tossed a football in the warm summer night. Another day at the fair drew to a close.

5

"Come a ki-yi-yippy, yippy yea . . ."

LaMona Pylman knelt beside Two-Eyed Roxie. In one hand she held a can of hoof-black polish and with the other she attempted to apply the blacking to the horse's hooves. Surrounded by strange noises and crowds, the horse refused to stand still. Each time LaMona daubed at a hoof, the horse moved, sidled, shied and otherwise proved cantankerous. By the time all four hooves were coated, there was a splotch inside Roxie's ankle, and LaMona looked as though she had strange measles.

She wiped away the smudge with a soapy cloth, and her younger brother, Kurt, led Roxie off to the show ring. LaMona looked down at her arms and groaned: "These spots will need a lot more scrubbing."

There were horse shows every day at the fair. In the hippodrome (a large, barnlike building with high arched roof, central arena and bleachers) the shows began at nine o'clock most mornings. They went on until at least nine at night. The first three days, the Morgan, pinto, paint, American saddle, Arabian, half-Arabian and Appaloosa horses paraded. After that came the quarter horses, palominos and draft horses. Always there were ponies.

LaMona, fifteen, poised and blond, had been at the barn since seven-thirty that morning. She had already walked one horse, Roxie. And her own horse, Chubby's Doll, had been vacuumed (to remove the dust) and brushed (to make her coat shine). "You can tell when they like the vacuuming," one boy said; "their nose starts going and they start leaning toward you." All the horses had been fed and watered early.

"I've traveled to horse shows with Dolly all summer," said LaMona, calling the horse by nickname. "I love it, going to the shows. It's better to do on weekends than stay home or just go downtown and goof around. You meet lots of kids at the shows. Sometimes we all get together and go to a movie or dance. It depends on how busy and how tired everybody is. I've been here all week and, oh, it's getting to be a long week. . . . But it's State Fair, and you get to talking to people and you go down to the midway and meet everybody.

"Last night there wasn't any competition, because they were taking horses out and bringing others in, so some of the people around the barns got together for some jackpotting. That's when they ante money into a pot and try calf roping—for the fun of it. I was the timer. After that they all decided to go for

62

some steer roping, nothing organized, just for the fun—because it's fairtime."

Horse show competition at the fair was open to anyone—with no special 4-H division. The 4-H horse competition has grown so large that it had been held earlier in the month. However, LaMona and Kurt, both 4-H members, had calves in the 4-H competitions at the fair. "We brought them Tuesday and showed them Friday. Kurt got a blue," LaMona made a face and laughed, "and I got a red." She was scheduled for a 4-H talk on (what else?) "Horse Showmanship," and her horse show competition would be the following day. LaMona has ridden horses since she was two or three, she really can't remember. Being around horses seems natural.

"I'll be nervous if it's a big class," she says, thinking of the show, "or when it's really important. Last year I got second. The class depends on the age of your horse—junior is four years and under, senior is five years and older. I'll be in the Quarter Horse Senior Western Pleasure class.

"Dolly's a fast horse, and before a show you have to ride her down a bit. She doesn't like it in the hippodrome, because when the people walk along the bleachers they scuffle their feet, and the sound makes her nervous.

"In the ring you concentrate on the horse's performance and on your riding—although here at the State Fair the judging is just on the horse, how it rides, how smooth it is, and not the rider's ability. Otherwise I'd enter a showmanship class. Mostly, I'll have to keep Dolly slowed down. She gets nervous when horses come up behind her, and she wants to go faster than the other horses.

"In competition the horses circle and reverse, walk, jog, lope and jogtrot. Then the judge asks you to line up and to walk toward him and to trot away from him. They look for good conformation—a horse with good muscling in the hindquarters and front quarters, a well-balanced horse. Showing a quarter horse, you don't get the horse to stretch like the Arabians do. You want them to stand square. I've been showing for three years, and it feels right if the horse is lined up right.

"This year Dolly has become sort of sour, and frequently when we walked up to the judge she'd rear as if something scared her. She'd jump up and goof around, and on the way back she'd lope instead of trot. There's nothing really to do about it, just be ready for it and bring her back into order."

During the summer, LaMona works out her horse for an hour or two each day. Some of the shows she enters are a distance to travel. Fort Robinson, Nebraska, is about 500 miles from her home, and Rapid City is 360 miles away. At the shows she earns state and national points, which are recorded with the Quarter Horse Association. (She is a junior director of her state group.) This point total determines who will represent the state at the national youth finals. LaMona and Dolly had qualified for the finals held in Tulsa, Oklahoma, the year earlier. Competing against forty-five in her division, LaMona placed fifth.

"I didn't qualify this year," she says; "I didn't show Dolly as much because she was too fat. She has a colt coming in

March and she looked too pregnant to take her to a national show. I'll ride her until the last show in November and then take her to Grandpa's. He has land in the western part of the state. The finals were fun—really exciting—there were kids there from all over."

Even during the winter LaMona enjoys competition. Last year it was basketball. "I played guard on the girls' junior varsity basketball team. But we used to practice every day after school until six and then I'd work the horse out in the riding ring for an hour and it was maybe seven-thirty when I got home—with homework still to do. My folks thought I was too busy, so this year basketball is out. The other day, though, I went into the gym and shot some baskets. I shouldn't have done it—I really miss it. Maybe next year I'll try out for the girls' basketball cheerleading squad—to encourage the girls' team. I'm hoping to take piano lessons again this year and that will mean daily practice. And I'm going to work at the hospital as a candy striper—two hours a week, one night after school. I've been thinking of nursing as a career, and I want to see if I like it."

The next day LaMona got ready for the horse show. She dressed "western" to the hilt: white felt hat with a pheasant feather, blue checkered shirt, white cowhide chaps with *LaMona* stamped all along one side and *Pylman* down the other. Her long blond hair hung in a single braid, swinging against her back, clipped at the top with a silver barrette.

"Got this barrette once when we were on a trip to a horse

LaMona Pylman and her quarter horse, Dolly, relax under the shade trees before their ring competition. LaMona's flashy chaps were a Christmas gift.

show. My folks thought I paid too much for it, but I love it," she said, touching it lightly as though for luck. Her red-white-and-blue belt buckle was a prize from a show at Fort Robinson. Her name was tooled across the back of her belt, too. She couldn't have gotten lost if she'd tried.

LaMona and Dolly were in a class of twenty-seven riders, circling the ring, walking and spacing themselves. LaMona was solemn, watchful of Dolly's moods. The competition went

66

quickly, as the judge studied each horse in turn. Then six horses were awarded ribbons for the class, but not Dolly. Even so, LaMona smiled as she rode out of the barn into the dazzling sunshine. "Feels good to be out of the ring," she said, "it was so hot in there." If she was disappointed, she took it in stride. There would be other shows.

To meet her schedule of summer horse-show competitions, LaMona works out on her horse for an hour or two each day. In the ring the horses are to circle while walking, then are asked to jog, lope and jogtrot.

LaMona rolled the chaps up over her boot fronts so they wouldn't drag on the barn floor and led Dolly back to her stall. She patted the horse. "I'll be back. I just want to get into my blue jeans."

Besides western competition, you could watch English riding events and teams of massive draft horses—with bucket-sized feet, thick-muscled necks. Some wore roses braided into their manes. The draft horses were judged as teams, in pairs, or singly, often drawing carts and buckboards. One horse was led in competition by a boy of eight, who stood scarcely belly tall beside it.

There were also costume events. In one competition, riders were dressed in Indian regalia and had to submit a short script describing their costume or some area of Indian tradition. When a young girl in fringed buckskin entered the ring on a pinto, a woman in the bleachers leaned forward eagerly. "I made that little girl's costume," she explained to the person beside her. "I'm Sioux, and that's authentic—the right shade of buckskin, the right beading. I didn't have to research it either."

When you tired of sitting in the bleachers, you could visit the stalls behind the arena and watch horses being groomed. You could mosey through outdoor stalls in front of the hippodrome, or through the horse barns behind it. All around the grounds, people rode and exercised horses. Youngsters rode for the fun of it in early morning and evening, sitting double and bareback.

Not far from the hippodrome, open-class sheep competition

was in full swing. Jodi was there watching her older brother show Southdowns and Shropshires. She had even helped show one group of sheep—handling 125 pounds of darting, devilish energy. "You have to get a good hold of their throat," she explained, gesturing, "and another back here—on the rump—and hang on to them. Make them stand." Jodi decided, "I'd rather show Rosie, because there's action to it." Rosie was in her stall recovering from another bath.

Walking toward the barns, you might have noticed a carefree figure leaning against a soft-drink stand—a dark-haired boy talking to two girls. Marty was still going strong.

Another group gathered at the dairy barn. Shelly and 4-H members from her home county were meeting with their extension agent, a trained agricultural adviser.

"We're going to review what you've studied about dairy cattle," he told them, "before your judging competition begins. Let's go through the barn and talk cattle." And they did—for nearly an hour.

"Whatever catches your eye first about the cow," he said, "put down a note about it to help you picture the animal a half hour later when you're marking cards and giving reasons for your choice to the judges. Now here's a cow that's dairy from one end to the other—good feet and legs and good mammary system. When you're judging . . ."

Shelly was taking deep gulps of air. "Ohhh, I'm nervous," she whispered to a girl standing near her. "This is as bad as cooking."

Jodi Liebnow visits the open sheep competition while her older brother competes.

"You'll have five classes," the farm agent went on, "and fifteen minutes per class. You'll fill out charts and give your reasons orally—so you'd better know what you're talking about. Think about good grammar when you're writing and speaking. In the Guernsey class, look for a pretty animal—but don't use the word *pretty* in your reasons. . . ."

"How about *stylish*?" asked Shelly.

"Yes, that's good," said the agent.

After the judging event, Shelly had just time to race back to the dorm and roll up her sleeping bag. The family loaded everything into the camper for their eight-and-a-half-hour trip across the state to home. "Ohhh, I wanted to hear the country western show tonight," Shelly sighed. "It's my favorite. But we've got to go home." She leaned out the camper window for a last look at the fair and a good-bye wave.

As Shelly's visit to the fair ended, another 4-H'er's began. Enter John Wheeting—earnest, dark-haired, brown-eyed, eleven years old and ready for action. He brought a saddle, a stiff rope and a steel "calf." They were props for his talk, "Rope That Calf."

"Could I please give my demonstration outdoors?" he asked the judge. Yes, he could. So John carried out two folding chairs, while his father hauled the saddle and the "calf." His mother followed with the rope, bridle and John's demonstration cards. His friend toted out a card table. John opened and saddled the chairs, pastured the calf (which he had made) some distance away and propped up the cards. He began by describ-

John Wheeting shows calf-roping techniques during his 4-H demonstration. Lassoing needs a stiff rope and straight aim.

ing his equipment, all necessary for roping a calf, and the roping technique.

By now people were stopping along the sidewalk to watch. Three men in cowboy garb paused, one surprised, one grinning and one baffled.

"I may not get it the first time," John said looking in the judge's direction; "I'm a little nervous." He twirled the rope overhead and let fly. He missed. He frowned, recoiled the rope, tried again—and this time the loop fell neatly over one end of the calf. Whichever end he caught, John was satisfied.

Later he said, "I have roped real calves, but I didn't get *them* the first time either. We don't have calves at home, so I mostly practice on my sheep." He owns eleven of them—probably very angry sheep.

"I've had to buy all of them," he said, "but now I have a buck and so I'll breed them at home. I want to build up my flock. I showed market ewes at the county fair and sold them there." After settling his expenses, his profit went toward paying his folks back for his motorcycle.

"It's a Chaparral, only an 80," he said. "My cousin lives a mile away and he's got a Honda 50, and we ride all over the place. Till we get older though, we have to ride in the ditches. I have grandparents and cousins on all sides of me, up and down the road. And I go to another cousin's, six miles away, to go swimming. They have this silo bottom, which is about six feet deep and about fifteen feet across, and they fill that with water and have a filter and we swim there."

Besides riding his motorcycle, John favors horseback riding. "I belong to two 4-H clubs, one is strictly a horse club. I showed at the state 4-H horse show—it's earlier than the fair. I got a blue ribbon there. About sixty kids competed, first in heats and then in the championship.

"I did a stock seat, where you walk, trot and canter around the ring and you're judged on your feet, seat and hands, and how you stop your horse. In English you post up and down at the trot, but in western you try and stick to the saddle. In a competition you have to be relaxed. If you're all tensed up, the horse can feel it and get nervous. You have to be ready for anything. If you're cantering and the judge tells you to stop fast, you have to be ready to do it right. It used to make me really nervous, but now it's not so bad."

Like LaMona, John traveled to horse shows during the summer. "My favorite is a five-day quarter-horse show down by Chamberlain—moving to a different town every day. I take my horse, Set Up Poco, and I do barrels and poles and stock seat.

"Barrels competition is set up like this. . . ." He marked a triangle. "You ride in and circle either the right or left barrel, then the second barrel, and then circle the far barrel, like a cloverleaf. It's timed, and the quickest time wins.

"With poles, you have six poles in a row. You run your horse straight down one side, then come back, weaving in and out of the poles. You turn him and come through again, then bring him straight home as fast as you can!

"I try to ride him every day, but sometimes I don't get it

done. You know, there are lots of kids in our school in town who have never ridden a horse! I was riding when I was three and a half, on a little Shetland pony about that tall. Didn't have a saddle or anything, just rode bareback with a piece of twine tied on the neck. I've never taken lessons, but my sister is teaching our cousins, and I help her."

John was also interested in the 4-H rodeos. The state finals were held the week before the fair. "They have steer-calf riding and goat tying for the junior kids," John said, "and riding bulls and saddle broncs for the seniors. At some of the kids' rodeos, kids under six ride sheep." Those sheep must be ready for anything.

By the time the sky turned to sunset shades, a fashion show opened outside the 4-H dorm. The audience sat on folding chairs or blankets or patches of grass. For an hour teenage girls paraded across the stage in outfits which they had made. There were jumpsuits, pantsuits, formals, culottes, capes, even blue jeans in the review. Some of the girls walked shyly across the platform, others smiled and paused and pivoted to show their outfits. Everyone got applause from some pocket of the audience—wherever family or friends or 4-H members from their home county gathered.

When the dress review ended, the audience drifted off toward the swirling lights and sounds of the midway, toward a beauty pageant in another hall, to the rodeo, or the hippodrome.

For the 4-H'ers there was another choice. This night the long dining hall was cleared of tables. A rock band strummed and wailed and thumped. Lights flashed red, green, blue . . . and the music grew. Wall-to-wall teenagers danced the latest fast and slow steps.

"It was a good band and mobs of kids," LaMona said later, "lots of fun."

6

"Where the lemonade springs and the bluebird sings . . ."

During the State Fair, the carnival midway was busy by ten o'clock each morning. Rides creaked into gear and the organ music began. Kids dawdled at the booths, staring at glassy-eyed panda bears, who stared back. Sooner or later everyone visited the carnival, set in the middle of the exhibit halls and food stands and machinery displays.

"My favorite time is when it opens, when the people start to come," says Dawn Payne. She knows the carnival firsthand—sees it when it opens, when it closes, when it's put up and taken down, when it's on the road. Dawn, who is ten, travels with the carnival.

Just as farming is a tradition for some families, the carnival is a tradition for Dawn's. Her mother traveled with it as a girl. So did her grandfather as a boy—when his uncle owned it. Now it belongs to Dawn's grandfather.

Summertime for her is a long meandering from town to town—the carnival moves from the Gulf of Mexico to the Rockies in Canada. From the end of April to the first week of October, the carnival covers twelve thousand miles. It plays thirty fairs and engagements each season.

"I love it!" says Dawn. "When we're in school and when spring starts, the rest of the carnival leaves—except for my mom and my sister and me. But as soon as we get out of school, we leave!" Her slim face, dusted with freckles, beams and she nods happily.

Even when she's in school Dawn remembers the carnival and her travels with it. Sometimes she writes stories about places she has visited in the summer. Her favorite places? "Well, there's Duluth [Minnesota] and Thunder Bay [Ontario, Canada] and Great Falls [Montana], because I got my dog there." She casts her eyes upward, remembering other favorites. "There's Butte [Montana] and Pierre [South Dakota] and Saskatoon [Saskatchewan, Canada]." She rolls the names along her tongue.

Dawn spends most of July in Canada. "Once a deer jumped right out on the road, and once there were three moose—no, four—a poppa, momma and baby that were crossing the road and one in the ditch.

"From Thunder Bay to Saskatoon"—Dawn says it like a line of poetry—"that takes three days. Sometimes, like then, I fly with Grandpa to long spots. He flies his own plane that carries five people."

78

On the road, Dawn and her parents and little sister Lisa live in a mobile home, towed by a pickup truck. At each stop Dawn is surrounded by cousins, aunts, uncles and, of course, her grandparents. Everyone is busy with the business of carnival.

Dawn helps, too. She works at various jobs—no set routine—trying her hand where she can. "I've worked in the joints, those are the game booths—like the monkey game and the water game." In both games, players shoot water at targets to make them race to the finish. "We run it," Dawn explains, "we take the coupons and start the game. My friend Shelly sometimes works in the balloon joint where you throw the darts; it's where her folks work.

"I've helped at selling in the poppers—the popcorn stands. And I put apples on sticks and dip them; but that caramel pops, and it can burn your arm! Sometimes I run up cotton candy from the machine.

"Another thing I did this summer was the balloons. You take two balloons—one is a Mickey Mouse—and you stuff it into this other balloon, you just poke it in there. And when you blow it up, first you blow up the balloon on the outside, then you blow up the one on the inside and it becomes a mouse." Dawn held the balloons while her mother operated the air tank, but next season she may learn to use the tank herself. Meanwhile, if she didn't hold tight, it was good-bye Mickey Mouse.

"Some popped because the air went in too fast, or too much," she says, "and you know, in the morning, after the balloons stay up for about half an hour, then the whole thing

Dawn Payne and her traveling dog, Princess, see a lot of country together on the carnival circuit. "Only if it rains," she says, "I stay indoors and read."

Dawn climbs the carnival equipment as naturally as a 4-H'er climbs a haymow. "Takes a long time to load up the carnival rides," she says.

gets blurry." Mickey stays fogged in until the air inside the balloon warms and clears again.

Besides working wherever she can, Dawn and her cousins and friends on the carnival, like hundreds of other kids, try all the rides. For free! "I haven't ridden every one," Dawn admits. "I like the big double Ferris wheel—it tickles my stomach. It feels like you're stuck on top, and it's as big as a house." Bigger.

"My favorite ride? The first one is the Spider . . . then the Tip Top, that zips around and makes a sound and goes up. And of the sideshows, I like the lizard best. We used to have a rat show that I didn't like; but I like the lizard, because it's interesting and you can ask questions about it. It's about this long. . . ." Dawn measured off about four feet. "Five feet," she guessed. "It has sharp claws, but doesn't have ears. They hear out of their tongue. One time the lizard came right up to me and I petted it. Felt bumpy like an alligator. Know how you can tell when they're hungry? When their stomach is up a little, a ways off the ground. That lizard eats fast, too." Dawn slid into a carnival spiel: "It eats rats, mice, dogs, cats, girls and boys. . . ."

Once a fair ends, it takes a day to break the carnival down and load and get on the road to the next destination. Because Dawn's father is in charge of the electrical equipment, she and her family are usually among the last on the road. "Once," said Dawn, "part of the Flying Bobs ride went right in the ditch. This one car just pulled them off the road. And another time going to Butte, part of the Sky Wheel tipped over. It took a long time to reload it."

Dawn was in Thunder Bay on her birthday. Although a carnival seems a perfect place for a birthday, Dawn was particularly happy because . . . "I got a bike!" The bicycle traveled with her, in the back of the pickup.

When they're not on the road, Dawn and her family live in a small town—in a big white house with a long porch across the front. It's where Dawn can have Halloween parties and play with her dog Princess, a miniature collie with teeth like thumbtacks. "We got her in Great Falls," said Dawn. "I'm going to take her with us next summer."

But for this summer, Dawn's travels were over. Her next stop was school and the fourth grade. In fact, she left the State Fair before many of the 4-H'ers—because she was invited to spend a weekend on a farm. "I always like to visit the animals at a fair," she explained, "and to see them on a farm, too. Once on my friend's farm, I was there when the sow had piglets! Sometimes I think I'll be a farmer; but then at school I do art, because I might grow up to be an artist."

Dawn paused and looked down at her cowboy boots from Montana. It would feel good to be home again. But by spring those feet would be itching to get back on the carnival circuit.

Her grandfather, Bernard Thomas, has owned the carnival for twenty-five years. Tall and tanned, he supervises the work of setting up, which takes a full day, and makes the plans needed to move a carnival all about the country. During the season the carnival may employ three hundred persons.

"Carnival has changed since I was a boy," he says. "Rides are more exotic and more popular. I think it's because you buy a ticket and you participate and everyone likes that. Even though we add new rides each year, the favorites are still the merry-go-round and the Ferris wheel. Today there are fewer sideshows, probably because of television—carnivals can't stage huge productions as TV can, so most carnivals have just a few sideshows."

During the off-season he travels to fair and carnival conventions in many states to line up bookings for the coming season. And there is enough maintenance and repair work to keep eight to twelve men busy during the winter months.

"What I miss," said Dawn's aunt, Margaret Atkins, "is playing the small towns where we set up on the main street. You really got to see the towns and what was going on. Nowadays, carnivals are usually stationed on fairgrounds on the edge of town, and that doesn't have the same excitement as setting up in the heart of town.

"We—my sisters and cousins and I—used to have contests to see who could stay on the rides the longest. Have you ever had twelve rides on a Tilt-a-Whirl? We had lots of friends that we'd see each summer, playing the same towns—mostly children of fair managers, or people connected with the fairground."

At one of the game booths, a boy of thirteen waited with fishing pole in hand. Inside the booth, a circular stream of water carried plastic bobbers swirling round and round. At the end of the fishline was a magnet, and on each bobber was a paper clip, and the object was to "fish" out a yellow bobber for a prize. White ones didn't count. The boy held his fishline steady, barely three inches over the bobbers. He waited. White and yellow sailed past. He waited. The water bubbled and rushed along. He waited. People stopped to watch, but he did not look up. The bobbers circled, and circled again. He waited. And then! The fishline dipped just once and came up with a catch—a yellow bobber. The boy chose a stuffed dog with a grin as wide as his own.

If you lost a game, you could console yourself with freshly squeezed lemonade, or a bag of salty popcorn, or a hot dog on a stick. Dawn's great-aunt Pauline Morton owned four "poppers" at the fair. A popper sells caramel apples dipped in nuts, and candy corn and juicy snow cones and—the all-time favorite—cotton candy.

"Cotton candy is such an American treat," said Mrs. Morton. "Everyone loves it. But the adults won't admit they like it. They ask for a bag of it to take home to their children—and you know they're going right home and eat it themselves!

"Cotton candy is made of sugar. Extreme heat in the machine melts the sugar and the coloring together. Then it is spun out through a wide webbing we call the ribbon. Comes out as wispy as a spider's web. On very busy days a single popper may use a hundred pounds of sugar."

Wherever the carnival moves, there are some jobs for local

Fluffy, sticky, delicious cotton candy. Imagine a fair
without it. Debbie earns college money traveling with
this "popper" on the fair circuit.

teens. Usually they are advertised in a local newspaper or with the state employment office. The jobs may involve working with the poppers, or with the carnival rides and games.

The fair board also hires workers—cleanup crews for the grounds and grandstand, ticket takers and sellers, grandstand usherettes, even "mounted parkers"—horseback riders who direct parking. Community and church groups open lunch counters and dining halls, which hire staff for fair week. The jobs get snapped up.

Jodi Hegg had waited impatiently all summer for her fourteenth birthday, when she would be old enough for a job. "Besides," she said, "I wanted to be fourteen because that's more teenage than thirteen." The magic number arrived just at fairtime and Jodi got her first job—at a lunch stand on the midway. Each afternoon at four o'clock she tied an apron over her blue jeans, slid a pencil behind her ear and began work. Until eleven or twelve o'clock at night, and sometimes one in the morning, she and the other waitresses balanced cups and plates, hoping not to spill anything as they squeezed past each other in the narrow service space. When the stand closed, Jodi's employer drove everyone home.

"The fair ends Monday night," she said, "and schools here open Tuesday. Think how tired I'll be!" As the week wore on, the slender, long-legged teen slept later each morning, and her collection of stuffed animals lay in a tumble beside her bed. She'd pick them up "next week."

Still, Jodi tackled the project with enthusiasm. "One of my

86

Jodi Hegg saw enough chili dogs to last her for weeks—while serving hundreds of them to fair visitors. Local schools open after the fair, so Jodi and her friends can earn some late-summer money.

friends was hired to wear a costume—a big rabbit suit—and walk around the fair talking to little kids. But it was so hot in that costume, she got another job.

"I'm putting all the money I earn into the bank, that's what I do with whatever I earn—baby-sitting or taking care of my grandparents' lawn or whatever. I'm saving for college. I'm going to study pharmacy like my sister."

Not only did her birthday mark the time she could work, but also the moment Jodi got a driver's permit. This allowed her to drive an automobile alone between the hours of seven in the morning and seven at night—just enough time after supper for one last trip to the local drive-in for a root beer float or a banana split.

Working at the fair meant Jodi missed one school activity. "Girls' basketball starts this week," she said thoughtfully, "but you have to make all the practices to be on the team, and there's even a game this week. I couldn't do everything. Later, I can go out for track: running and high jumping."

All fair week Jodi and her friends looked forward to attending the Midnight Special on Sunday in the grandstand. It was to be a rock concert, and tickets cost five dollars—if you could get one. The biggest problem was convincing a parent to drive them home at three in the morning when it was over.

Sunday is a big day at a state fair. Farmers don't farm. Stores are closed. Schools are out. Everyone heads for the fair. Lines queue at the lemonade stand and the bumper car amusement. Tacos and pizza and corn on the cob sell like hotcakes—and one booth even sells hotcakes. An open-air "railroad" pulled by tractor hauls people from the east side of the fairgrounds to the west side and people from the west side to the east. Everyone wants to try everything.

The 4-H activities continued. Marty tilted his hat at a jaunty angle as he entered the junior livestock-judging contest. This group judged market lambs, market steers, Angus breeding cattle and market hogs—sixteen head in all. They had twelve minutes for each category. Marty looked carefully at the animals in each pen, to choose the best example of each and to give his reasons. He moved about to see them from all angles, comparing, thinking, checking his card for the judges. He finished ahead of time, turned in the card and headed toward the midway.

By evening the double Ferris wheel had probably revolved seven hundred times. Merry-go-round horses still jumped their invisible hedges, balloons popped at the dart game and a bingo announcer cried, "Under *B*, 17."

On this particular night Dawn was not watching the people and the lights. She was listening to crickets on her friend's farm.

But Jodi Hegg was in the thick of the activity, dishing up hot dogs and chili dogs, pouring coffee and cold pop and serving ice cream and adding the bills and making change and cleaning the counter and hoping she wouldn't forget anything and wondering if she could leave in time for that midnight show.

Marty and a friend meandered past her stand, making their

Over 200 junior livestock judges try their skill at choosing
the best of the bunch. Marty Pearson, center, gives his
attention to the livestock in the ring.

way from the band shell of blue-grass music to the band shell with a free rock show. Even though the rock show repeated four times a day, the sides of the stage were filled an hour early by teenage girls waiting for the group to go on.

On the midway, between a costume-jewelry stand and a hats-and-belts booth, a black-and-white puppy darted this way and that. He chased a scrap of paper and followed an interesting foot. But whoever had chosen him from the animal nursery had lost him here among the rushing crowd.

7

"Fare thee well . . ."

Even on the last morning of the fair, the barns were busy by seven o'clock. Livestock must be fed—twice a day, at that. Some 4-H members brushed their animals to tidy them for sale, but the blowing and polishing and tail fluffing were missing. The steel cattle stalls were empty, except for the boys chinning one-handed on them. Girls sitting nearby were careful not to notice.

A six-year-old tagged after a sixteen-year-old. "Can I help you feed your calves?"

"Sure, why not. Here's a bucket—the water's that way." The little boy dashed off, bucket thumping against his leg.

"Got an idea," said one teen to another, "next year I'll bring my steels and you bring yours and . . . wouldn't it be neat if our bands could get together!"

A girl sitting cross-legged on a bale claimed, "All you had to do was throw a couple darts to win a big panda."

"Where's the panda?"

"Otherwise you got this. . . ." She opened her hand to reveal a red plastic bear.

Between the rows of pens, little kids played their favorite game: Jump-in-the-aisles-and-see-how-much-dust-you-can-raise.

There were blue jeans as far as the eye could see. And T-shirts which read "I'm proud to be a farmer's daughter," or "State Bird," under the picture of a giant mosquito.

The most noticeable fashion trend was the new shape for cowboy hats—best called "the droop." Take the usual big-brimmed hat and steam the brim—so it collapses wide on each side. Roll just the hint of a curl at the outer edges. Then flatten the front and back brims so they dip as low as possible. Now tie on a band of beads. Or add pheasant feathers. Or a peacock plume that trails eighteen inches behind the hat. Put it *all* on. Now that's a hat worth crowing about.

The last morning, in place of the usual cattle being bathed, a black-and-gray dog was tied near a spigot. In spite of the sunny morning, he was shivering. He was also sopping wet from being shampooed and rinsed. Just when he seemed to be finished, his owner poured a cream rinse over his coat. "Helps make it glossy," she explained. The dog was rinsed again and toweled and brushed. Another 4-H competition would begin in an hour.

A small bleacher had been erected, and the lawn in front of the dormitory had gone to the dogs. Compared with the other livestock, the dog show is a new 4-H project. It is not a best-of-

A new variation of an old favorite—the western hat. Steam the brim so it's wide at the sides and dipped front and back, then add a feather.

breed type show, in fact some of the breeds are beyond identification. The purpose of the project is obedience training and showing the dog.

Some pets were still being brushed and talked to in sweet tones as the competition began. The dogs were to heel, sit and stay. Each was to sit quietly as the judge looked at its coat, ears and paws.

94

The black-and-gray dog, a part-English setter named Bouncer, was an early entry. He walked properly and was rewarded with pats. But he didn't see the point of standing when it was so pleasant to sit.

The collie that followed looked insulted when the judge inspected his ears, but he wagged his tail gamely. It took a feisty little mutt to show what he really thought of the event—by nipping the judge. The judge glared as though she might bite back.

At the rear of the cattle barn an auctioneer's chant rose and fell in a steady drone—the 4-H livestock sale was underway. One at a time, members led their beef into the auction ring to be sold. Most of the stock was purchased by meat-packing plants. Another auction sale began in the sheep-swine arena.

There were many somber faces. Neal had said, "You get sort of attached to the animals. You spend so much time on them."

And John remembered, "Charlie was the name of the first lamb I ever brought to the State Fair. That was hard, that sale. Every year my flock has one Charlie in it."

In the swine barn, one pig basked in attention. On his back were a purple ribbon and two blue ones. Behind him stood his owner, nine-year-old Michael Rusten, looking sober but determined. Beside him was his brother Timothy, four, close to tears—again. All three were being photographed.

"It's just like selling a member of the family," said the boys' mother. "Michael has worked with him every day. He's reconciled to selling; but not Timothy. I don't know what he'll do

95

when that pig comes into the sale ring."

The auctioneer lost no time on any of the pigs. It took less than sixty seconds to complete a sale. Each pig was herded into a pen for loading onto trucks for the slaughterhouses. Only a few pigs were bought by breeders.

Neal sold his pigs for forty-two cents a pound, about $109 each. When he asked for "cutout data," he was disappointed that the stockyard buyer said it wouldn't be possible to tell him how it "dressed out," that is, how the carcass rated in terms of lean and fat. Marty brought a pig into the ring and sold it for about $120. That should help trim the feed bill.

As the sale went on, Michael's mother and young Timothy waited. It was Michael's first year in 4-H and at the State Fair. He had raised this pig from his own brood sow's litter. The money would be his—for his savings account and for school clothing.

"The children buy their own clothes," his mother said, "I help with some decisions, but as few as possible. It's good training for them to handle their own money."

Suddenly it was Michael's turn. He herded the pig into the small triangular area, and the auctioneer opened the bidding. Timothy darted forward to the fence and dropped to his knees. Gently he reached through the wire and patted the pig . . . whispered something to it. And just as quickly it was sold, and Michael shooed it toward the loading pen.

Timothy stood up and turned to his mother, who was holding her breath. Unexpectedly he smiled, as if to say, "That was a terrific pig, wasn't it!"

While the auctioneer chants, Timothy Rusten says a soft good-bye
to his brother's pig at the 4-H livestock sale.

But if there was drama in the sales ring, there was one animal enjoying herself and spending a quiet morning meditating in the dairy barn. Rosie didn't even regret missing her morning bath. She lay chewing on alfalfa. That evening, Jodi and her parents would load Rosie and all the rabbits into a truck for the trip home. Jodi would miss the fair, but there would be all those new ribbons on her bedroom wall to help her remember the excitement—and to dream of next year.

Marty planned to collect his sheep in the late afternoon. Wouldn't be long though before he could load them up again for the 240-mile trip to Omaha—and the biggest 4-H livestock show of all.

What Marty didn't know—couldn't guess—was that the Ak-Sar-Ben would be a special thrill. Not only would his lambs place fourth and fifth—achievement enough—but his pig out of 451 entries would be the Grand Champion. Besides the title, that pig would earn $3,075 for Marty at the Ak-Sar-Ben live-stock sale. Ordinarily a 246-pound pig would sell to a meat packer for less than $150, but a grand champion on the way to market gets champion prices. Bidders such as Safeway Stores, who bought Marty's pig, pay top money for the prize animals to support the 4-H'ers' efforts and to encourage them to raise livestock. Mighty encouraging!

That was still to come. It had been a big week at the State Fair. "I'm okay here," Marty said with a grin and a shrug, "but when I get home I'll probably drop." The Midnight Special? "Yeah, saw that. Mostly western, and we left early." The 4-H dance? "Yeah, neat!" He covers a lot of ground. If you should

98

drive through the farm belt and see someone herding sheep on motorcycle—wave. It might be Marty.

In the hippodrome John Wheeting watched his sister compete in English equitation and waited for the pole-bending and barrel races to follow. On the sidelines, a girl, realizing at the last minute that she had to show a horse, grabbed the comb she'd been using on the horse and whisked it through her own hair before going into the ring.

Jodi Hegg's steps were slower as she arrived for work. She was not moving like a track hopeful. "We heard the entire Midnight Special," she explained. "I got home at four A.M." And? "It was all right. One group was country and the other was rock. I expected it way better.

"The fair's been great, though," she said firmly. "I liked the Rocko planes and the Zipper. And it was fun working here this summer. I'll do it again next year, I hope, but maybe I'll ask for different hours. The only thing that went wrong was . . . well . . . three people left without paying." She sighed. "Sometimes we'd get so busy . . ."

And so . . . the fair in the heart of the country came to a close. The wooden awnings at the lunch stands were bolted shut. The rodeo stock was trucked away to pasture until another celebration. Racing cars were loaded onto flatbed trailers. Hands knocked down the rides and wrapped the seats in tarps and coiled electrical wires. The carnival was bound for Spencer, Iowa, where one of the largest county fairs in the country was about to open.

Exhibit halls were cleared of green vegetables and plates of cookies and butterfly displays and macrame hangings and woolen coats and scrapbooks of wild grasses.

Boys with fishnets collected scraps of paper and empty Styrofoam cups from the grounds, and when the nets were full carried them to garbage bins. There were barns full of bedding straw to be scooped up and carted away. And in another month, the planning would begin again—for another fair the following fall. At harvest time. Come to the fair.

"Meet me at the fair . . ."

Wherever you live, you can enjoy a fair. This list tells where and when they occur. Most are state fairs, but a few local fairs are listed, too. Many have special events you won't want to miss. Because the dates change slightly each year, these are approximate. You can find exact dates in local newspapers.

Alabama: Ten days from first Thursday in October, Birmingham. Children's competition in cattle, swine, crafts.

Alaska: Eleven days, ending Labor Day, Palmer. Special fun: a greased-pole contest, three-legged race, bicycle marathon. Do see Colony Village, the seventy-pound cabbages, the decorated-egg exhibits.

Arizona: Early November, Phoenix.

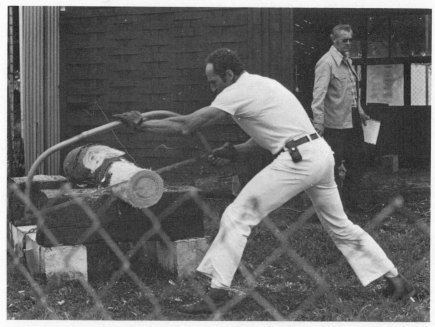

At the Danbury State Fair in Connecticut, lumberjacks demonstrate speed and skill with the tools of their trade, saws and axes.

Arkansas: Ten days, beginning last Friday of September, Little Rock. Busy and fun: the Children's Barnyard.

California: Twelve days, late August, Sacramento.

Colorado: Nine days ending Labor Day, Pueblo. Watch for butter-churning, hog-calling, rooster-crowing contests; doll exhibit.

102

Connecticut: Danbury State Fair, ten days, early October, Danbury. Lumberjack and ox-drawing competitions.

Delaware: Last full week of July, Harrington.

Florida: Twelve days, early February, Tampa.

Georgia: Six days, mid-October, Macon.

Hawaii: Fiftieth State Fair, first week of July, Honolulu. Favorites: hula dancing and island crafts.

Idaho: Western Idaho Fair, eight days ending Saturday before Labor Day, Boise. Enjoy the Children's Barnyard.

Illinois: Mid-August, Springfield.

Indiana: Ten days, late August, Indianapolis. Contests for high school marching bands, cheerleading, pet parades, 4-H horseshoe pitching.

Iowa: Ten days, mid-August, Des Moines. For fun: rooster-crowing, arm-wrestling, hog-calling, chicken-calling contests.

Kansas: Nine days, mid-September, Hutchinson. Pony-pulling events, 4-H sheep shearing, kids' barnyard.

Kentucky: Eleven days, mid-August, Louisville. Visit the rooster-crowing contest.

Louisiana: Ten days, October, Shreveport.

Maine: Pick from twenty-five local fairs! Mid-July through October. Youth activities: calf and pig scrambles, tractor driving. Fryeburg Fair has lumberjack competition in log-rolling, tree cutting, chain sawing; late September.

At the Michigan State Fair a visitor finds a competition she
can really sink her teeth into. (Michigan State Fair Photo)

Maryland: Ten days, begins late August through Labor Day weekend, Timonium. Special event: "Pretty Cow" contest.

Massachusetts: Eastern States Exposition, twelve days, including third week of September, West Springfield. Storrowton Village area has sheep shearing, oxcart rides, sack races, three-legged races. Visit the Avenue of States for homemade ice cream, apple cider, maple sugar.

Michigan: August, Detroit.

Minnesota: Twelve days, ending Labor Day, Saint Paul/Falcon Heights. Hog-calling, rooster-crowing, turkey-weight-guessing, horse-harnessing events. 4-H sponsors Art-in-the-Park.

Mississippi: Second week of October, Jackson.

Missouri: Nine days, mid-August, Sedalia. Motorcycle races.

Montana: Last week of July, first week of August, Great Falls. Features: International Cow Chip Throwing Contest. In Helena: Last Chance Stampede includes 4-H fair, four days, late July. Square dancing, fly casting, family team roping.

Nebraska: First week of September, Lincoln.

Nevada: First week of September, Reno. Wild 'n woolly rodeo.

New Hampshire: Enjoy thirteen local fairs, late July to mid-October. Popular contests: racing to win a pig, pie eating.

New Jersey: Ten days, begins Friday after Labor Day, Trenton. Special children's shows; rabbit and cavy exhibits, dairy goats.

The Spanish village at the New Mexico State Fair invites all comers to the daily piñata festivities. (Far West Photography)

New Mexico: Twelve days, mid-September, Albuquerque. Visit Indian and Spanish villages on fairgrounds. Try your hand at the daily piñata-breaking fun.

New York: Eight days, beginning Tuesday before Labor Day, Syracuse.

North Carolina: Nine days, third week of October, Raleigh.

Native American dancers are part of the color, sounds and excitement in Oklahoma City at fairtime. (Oklahoma State Fair Photo)

Don't miss: old log cabin and schoolhouse, antique farm machinery, junior dairy goat competition.

North Dakota: July, Minot.

Ohio: Last week of August, Columbus.

Oklahoma: Ten days, includes last week of September, Oklahoma City. Fun to see: American Indian ceremonial dances;

baton-twirling, pie-eating, fiddling and Christmas-tree-trimming contests.

Oregon: Nine days, ending on Labor Day, Salem. Enter a bubble-gum contest, pan-for-gold event, spelling bee. Visit the Animal Village.

Pennsylvania: Annual Farm Show, five days, mid-January, Harrisburg. Band concerts, 4-H exhibits, folk dancing.

Rhode Island: Rocky Hill State Fair, third week in August, East Greenwich.

South Carolina: Nine days, includes third week of October, Columbia. One event of junior dairy competition has animals in costumes. Special interest: milking parlor.

South Dakota: Six days ending Labor Day, Huron.

Tennessee: September, Nashville.

Texas: Mid-October, Dallas. Take a gondola ride over fairgrounds. Check out the four-story-tall cowboy figure.

Utah: Ten days, early September, Salt Lake City. Contests for freckles, pets and twins.

Vermont: Seven days, September, Rutland.

Virginia: Eleven days, late September, Richmond. Most fun: greased-pig-catching contest, tobacco-spitting contest, hog calling, milking parlor, majorette contest and circus.

Washington: Western Washington Fair, third week of September, Puyallup. Try your luck: scone-eating, pickle-eating contests. Watch the horseshoe-pitching tournament, logging

It's worth all the combing and brushing if you win a contest for the longest braids. A state fair has contests for everyone. (Wisconsin State Fair Photo)

rodeo. Enjoy Forest Products Day. Central Washington Fair, first week of October, Yakima. Visit MacDonald's Farm.

West Virginia: Eight days, mid-August, Lewisburg. Free: harness racing, circus, draft-horse-pulling contest.

Wisconsin: Eleven days, opens Thursday before second weekend of August, Milwaukee/West Allis. Favorite contests: freckles, look-alike twins, longest braids, funniest face.

Wyoming: Six days, late August, Douglas. Educational displays from schools of every county. Enjoy: kids' parade, junior tractor-driving contest.

CANADA

Alberta: Seven days, early November, Edmonton. Canadian National Finals Rodeo.

Eleven days, late July, Edmonton. Klondike Days Exposition (agricultural, household and commercial).

Ten days, July, Calgary. Exhibition and Stampede.

British Columbia: Four days, mid-August, Chilliwack. Enjoy: Indian arts, midway, livestock and horticultural displays.

Manitoba: Six days, mid-June, Brandon. Special attractions: Tractor pull, midway, livestock show and sale.

Five days, mid-July, Morris. See: Rodeo, bronc riding, chariot and running races, bull riding, steer wrestling.

Ontario: Twenty days, mid-August to early September, Toronto. Canadian National Exhibition, "oldest and largest annual exhibition in the world." Highlight: "World Tattoo" featuring bands from six countries.

Renfrew, dates not available. Don't miss: Rodeo, horse and cattle judging, handicraft exhibits and 4-H club exhibits.

Saskatchewan: Six days, early August, Regina. Enjoy: "Buffalo Buck Casino," AgriShow, band concerts, hobby displays and amateur sports.

Seven days, last week of March, Regina. See: Annual Regina Bull Show and Sale, Regina Light Horse Show, Agricultural show for Grade 3 students.

Seven days, usually last week in November, Regina. Canadian Western Agribition includes: Indoor rodeo and livestock exhibition and sale.

Format by Joyce Hopkins
Set in 12 pt. Video Times Roman
Composed by The Haddon Craftsmen, Scranton, Pa.
Printed by The Murray Printing Co.
Bound by The Haddon Craftsmen, Scranton, Pa.
HARPER & ROW, PUBLISHERS, INC.